Miss You Bruzzo

Glimpses of Childhood Memories

Miss You Bruzzo

Tanishi Sharma

Illustrations : Stuti Maheshwari

Editor : Amrendra Kumar

UNBOUND SCRIPT

UNBOUND SCRIPT

Miss You Bruzzo
ISBN : 978-93-92088-23-0
First Edition : 2022

Published by **Unbound script**
B-10, Seven Wonder Business Center
Plot No. G-20, Basement, Preet Vihar
New Delhi-110092

Website : www.unboundscript.com
Email : books@unboundscript.com
Printed in India

Price : 199/-

Miss You Bruzzo
by Tanishi Sharma
Illustration by Stuti Maheshwari

About the book

The book vividly depicts the feelings, imaginations and keen observations of a little girl who is fond of pets. Many a times, she asks her mamma for bringing a pet into the house. Her mamma however, refuses all the time. She doesn't budze an inch. In despair, the little girl finds a way out. She makes excuses to meet frequently a friend who has a parrot in her house. She spends a lot of time there and comes home back with a heavy heart.

One fine evening when she was about to finish her dinner, she heard the sound of meow-meow and found a cat in her balcony. Her delight was immense. Cat also didn't disappoint her. She continued to come to the balcony every late evening and stayed there for the whole night. She along with her grandpa made it a routine to give her milk secretly and enjoyed her lively presence in the balcony.

The happiness, however, didn't last for long. The little girl had to shift from the apartment life of the National Capital Region, Delhi to a calm and quiet place Dharamshala in Himachal Pradesh. For some days, the new city was boring. She was not happy. But, the scenic beauty of Dhauladhar ranges caught her sight and soon opened a new world to her. She developed a habit of bird watching in Dharamshala.

She was fortunate here. Along with bird watching, she keenly observed the activities of the owner's dog from her 1st-floor balcony. Slowly, she adventured to play with and developed friendship with the dog fondly called Bruzzo by his owner. She learned different shades of emotions that the pet exhibited in response to her gestures.

This came to be a great relief to her in the distressing time of pandemic COVID-19. She spent a lot of time learning about nature, which she was unfamiliar of while living in a metro city. She began to understand how a pet dog was trained to perform multitask. She found in Bruzzo a true friend who reciprocated love and feelings in abundance, but it also lasted only for a few months...

Acknowledgements

It is indeed pleasure to see the memoirs taking shape of the book. I am thankful to my teachers, friends and family members who have been encouraging me all along the journey. I am fond of stories since my childhood and have always been asking mamma, dadi and dada to tell me stories. Papa would also tell me several stories. It developed in me a habit of listening to stories from them and thereafter I would narrate the same to nani over the phone. The practice took me on the path of writing in distressing time of COVID 19 when school was closed. I thank all of them for supporting me.

I would also like to thank J N Sinha uncle and Hari uncle for reading the manuscript and giving valuable suggestions before publications. I owe my special thanks to Meetu Massi, Uncle and Aunty. The time I spent with Bruzzo is treasure for me. I thank my friends Chiya, Gurmannat, Ankita and the whole gang of Patrakar Vihar in Ghaziabad. My special thanks to Niharika and Atishi my friends in Dharamshala.

It was not possible to publish the book without the continuous encouragement and support of the publisher of the book Mr. Alind Maheshwari and his team as well. I owe lots of thanks to all of them and also to the creative illustrator Miss. Stuti Maheshwari and cover designer Mr. Suresh Panwar.

Yes... I also owe my thanks to all the characters of my book Bruzzo, Alex..., Munro... My special thanks goes to you, my dear readers...

Content

Get me a pet!

To play with a pet for a while has been one of my cravings. There were no animals or birds in my house. I lived in a flat not big enough to have pets. Despite the space problem, I always wanted to have a pet. I desired to spend my leisure time with them. Whenever I saw my friends or anybody in the apartment strolling with pet dog or a cat, my desire would increase manifold.

It was not easy to have though. There are many things one need to do in advance. Without thinking of problems, when I was sitting in my drawing room with mamma and grandma on Sunday, I expressed my desire to mamma. I had thought mamma was in a good mood.

I asked her, "Mamma, can we keep a dog as a pet?"

She responded immediately, "No, it is not possible. Our house is a small one."

Stunned to listen to her response, I thought for a moment and before making another request, I gathered my courage and said, "Please keep it, mamma. My other friends are managing in this space only."

She was quiet for a while that made me to say

something more.

I pleaded, “I need a dog. I want to play with it”.

She stares at me and said, “Will you be able to take care of the dog? Who will take him for a walk outside daily?”

“Mamma, I will do. I promise you. There will be no problem. I have spoken to Papa. He will help me. I along with papa have already seen the dog and also some lovely colorful birds.”

I said hurriedly to calm her. But, it was of no use. It made her rather angry and she was also not happy to know about my prior efforts.

She asked me, "Will you make it to have a bath? Who will clean his potty?" Without a pause, she went on asking a number of questions. She warned me, "You should know that I will not be able to handle the dog."

Just to interrupt her after listening long list of questions, I put another question jokingly.

I asked, "Can we keep a cat, mamma?"

She burst out hearing this. She started telling me. "You should know that I dislike cats. If a cat's hair is mixed with food, the whole food is wasted."

Puzzled to see her temper soar so high, I smiled and joked, "Mamma, why do not we keep a child of monkey or lion!" I knew well that keeping a wild animal in the home is not allowed. It is an offence. Mamma had told me earlier. These animals are kept in a zoo. Mamma did not respond to anything. I noticed a fishy look on her face. She got up and went straight to the kitchen. I felt very sad to know of her views.

Thereafter, I had been upset for whole day and my thought didn't go away from pet animals. Then a stunning incident happened the next day.

Cat in my balcony

I was not feeling better the following day. I was hurt. I was stirred from inside. It was surprising for me. I was not able to believe it. Mamma had refused my wishes without paying attention to my long cherished dream. How could she be so heartless?

I was trying to do something different to make my mood uplift. In daytime, after coming back to home from school, I tried to keep myself busy with my favorite cartoon shows. It helped a bit.

It was about nine o'clock in the night, I got a big surprise. I had gone to grandpa's room. My flat was on the ground floor in Patrakar Vihar society of Indirapuram, Ghaziabad in Uttar Pradesh. I was talking to grandpa about my friends. He had just come from the temple which was inside the society. My friends and I would play regularly nearby the temple. That day, I hadn't gone to play with them.

After talking for some time, I came back to the drawing-room. While I was sitting at the dining table and about to finish my dinner, the sound of meow-meow reached to my ears. I guessed that the sound was coming from my grandpa's room.

Excitedly, I ran to the room. When I looked around in grandpa's room and in the balcony, I found a white colour cat peeping towards the room. As soon as I looked outside at the cat, she crossed the other side through the gap of the grill in the balcony. Grandpa told me that the lovely cat used to come to the balcony every night.

I came to the kitchen and finding mamma not present there, I took two breads and poured milk in a bowl and brought it to the grandpa's room. I knew she would come again. I placed the bowl outside; I shut the door ajar to see the cat. I hid and waited till the cat turned up. I saw that she came in from space between the grills. Cat looked around with cautious eyes. She might be hungry. That's why she immediately started drinking milk. After drinking milk, she also ate bread. Then, she looked around here and there and after a short while lied down spreading her legs. I was enjoying a lot her activities.

The clock struck 11 when mamma called me. She came nearby and asked me to go to bed. I requested, "May I sleep along with Dadi today."

I was trying to ignore Mamma, which she noticed. She wanted me to be with her as the whole day she was in her office. It was only in the night we would get time to be together. She would feel relaxed talking to me for a while before sleeping.

She thought for a moment and said, "The whole day you live with grandma. It's already late. You go now and sleep."

I tried not to listen her. I was lost in the thought of cat. I knowingly annoyed her in the excitement of finding a new cat in the house.

My naughtiness came to an end when she yelled at me. She ordered me, "Get your bag and make it ready fast. You have to go to school tomorrow."

I nodded and moved out of grandpa's room. In the bed too, I was thinking about cat. When I woke up in the middle of the night, I rushed to the grandpa's balcony to have a look. Cat was there lying relaxed as I had left at 11 PM. Happily, I came back and didn't sleep thereafter. I got up early at six o'clock in the morning and waited for mamma to go to kitchen to get my lunch box ready.

When mamma went to the kitchen, I rushed to see the lovely cat. She had gone! I asked grandpa, "Where is the cat?" He said, "She will come again in the evening." I took a sigh of relief.

The longest day

It was the longest day for me. Every minute that passed, seemed to be an hour. Impatience loomed large over me. I wanted a time machine. I kept asking my grandpa, "How the cat used to come in the night?"

I asked grandpa, "Did he give her milk in the past?"

I felt at peace when my grandpa told that he used to give her bread from his meal occasionally.

"Yes," I exclaimed. She would come in the evening. I got overwhelmed.

The whole day I kept thinking about his return in the evening. The day long wait was not getting over. Now, it was half-past seven. Mamma was about to come home anytime from the office. I wanted to see the cat before she arrives. I had not eaten anything from my lunch box and kept it ready to give to the cat and see her eating.

Suddenly, I heard murmuring behind the curtain. It was she!

"Oh God, She has come."

I jumped, forgetting what to do next. In no time, I realized the cat had got scared and looked around to make sure nobody was present. Thankfully, she got settled in a minute time. I slowly opened the door and gave her bread. After two minutes, she started

to eat with caution. When she was looking the other side, I passed the bowl full of milk. She ran away at once. I got worried. But, what I saw after a few minutes was amazing. It was fun unlimited. I relished her way of sipping milk. Oh God, It was a real amazement.

Thereafter, it was a routine to me. Spending evening time with her every day was my pastime. She used to relish the food given by us and stayed at night and leave the balcony off in the morning and return to balcony around 8 p.m.

Sometimes, she came there for afternoon siesta. She was living in grandpa's balcony very comfortably. I and my grandpa would give bread, milk and biscuits as well. At times, she would get a piece of chocolate also from my side. Yes, she was not afraid to see me now. Probably, she might have started to accept my friendship.

After two months passed, I found that she had stopped coming to my balcony. As usual her food was kept but she did not come. When she did not turn up to our house for few days, I got worried. One day after coming from the school, I started searching for her in the entire society. I found that she had gone to stay in the small park next to our block.

Two days later, what I saw was that there were three small kittens with her. They were all white and black in color. Now I understood what the matter was. She wanted a more comfortable place than our balcony. She wanted to protect her kittens.

Our balcony could not have been a safe and secure place for them. People would always keep walking the other side of the balcony. Also, there were heap of dried grasses in the park. On the soft bed of the grasses, the three kittens were lying comfortably with their closed eyes. They were hardly moving.

When the cat was not around her kittens, I along with my friends would go near and rejoice seeing them and sometimes touch them softly. One day, my best friend Chiya was playing along with them. I came later and saw Chiya disturbing the cat. She wanted to see her kittens in the cat's presence. The cat didn't like her audacity and jumped at once upon her and scratched Chiya's hands. We got frightened and rushed to her mamma and told her about the incident.

Aunty scolded Chiya badly. Chiya was taken to the hospital then. When my mamma returned home in the evening, I was also warned and asked not to go near the cat and her little family. This incident, however, stopped us for a few days only. One day when we found the mother cat away, we started touching one kitten again and again. The cat saw this from distance.

What the mother cat did after that was a shock for all of us. She abandoned one of her kittens. I do not know why she had left her child! I was puzzled. To know about the truth, I revealed the secret to mamma. She didn't believe all this. She was stunned to know all this. But, mamma helped me overcome the shock. She said that when a human being touches children of an animal or bird, the human smell remains on them. They don't like that and so they abandon their children. Probably something similar might have happened to that kitten. The kitten left by the mother was in search of her food moving here and there. She met an unfortunate accident. She got hurt badly by the car coming from the front side and died after a short while. I felt pity.

The tragedy didn't end here. A few days later, the second kitten died due to an electric shock. What we saw after some days the mother also disappeared. I wanted to keep single left kitten with me, but mamma refused my request again. Sometimes I went to see it and gave food and milk. A few days later that kitten also disappeared. Clueless! Where she might have gone to? All these incidents occurred with such a speed that really made me scary.

Ankita's Parrot

It was difficult to fill the void created by the tragic end of the cat and it's newly born little kittens. I was feeling lonely and sad. Sometimes, I used to talk to my friend Ankita. She lived in another block. I would play games with her in the evening. We were very good friends. One day when the evening game was over, I was having a conversation with her. She said to me, "I am going to Varanasi where my Nana-Nani lives. I will come back after two weeks time spending with them."

It was a bit more depressing for me, as she was the only one with whom I would share my memories of the cat. Anyway, I had to accept it.

When she went to Varanasi, I however got along with other children of my age. After vacations, Ankita returned with a surprise. She called me out from the other side of the balcony. When I came outside she took me to her home. It was a pleasant surprise to see that she had brought two small chicks of parrot. I asked her, "How did you manage to bring chicks of parrot?"

Ankita said, "Oh yes. Surely, it was difficult to bring birds in the train."

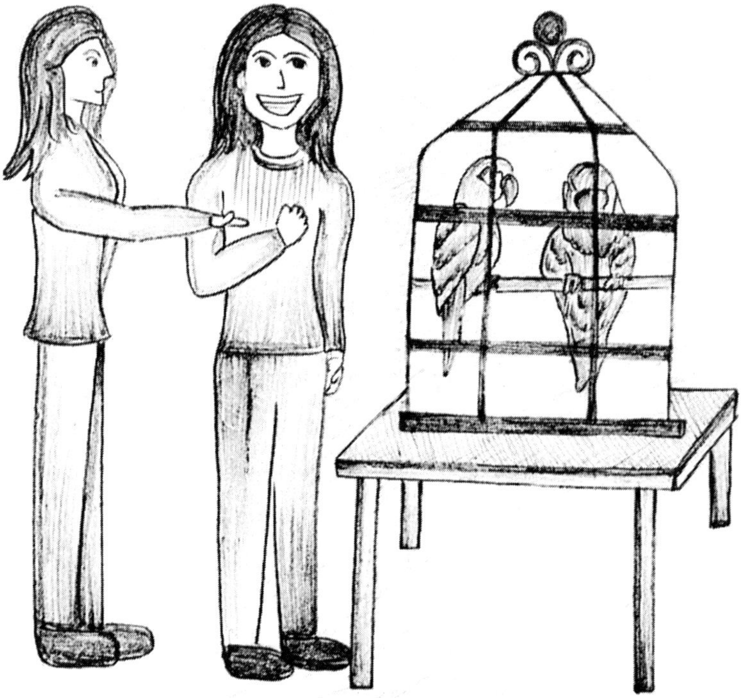

I was curious to know so I enquired putting many questions to her. She narrated me how she had managed to trick others in the train. She told me that the cage was covered well with clothes. The clothes were cut at several places, so that air continued to pass inside to breath. Then it was placed in a large luggage bag. The luggage bag was kept under the seat.

"Was the chain of the bag closed?" I eagerly asked her.

She said, "No, the chain was kept open and many holes were made in the bag as well, so that the parrots could get plenty of oxygen.

“Didn't people sitting next to your seat hear the sound of baby parrots?” I questioned her in curiosity.

Ankita answered, “No. Both are very small. They are unable to make loud sound. When the sound of their chirping became audible at times; we started singing a song loudly at the moment. Now you can see the two baby parrots are well living in my home Ghaziabad.”

Waving her hand proudly, Ankita said laughingly the story of parrot's journey from a holy city Varanasi to hugely polluted city Ghaziabad in the NCR Delhi. Parrots were quite small, punching their beak at the cage door. I felt that they were making efforts to get out.

I told Ankita, “Parrots do want to get out of the cage.” Ankita said, “Yes, they are new to this. They are not akin to this sort of living. They want to fly out of the cage.”

She further said that they were very naughty. She added, “You know, in the morning, mamma put her palm inside the cage to feed them some grains. They had full of tummy but one of them attacked and bite mamma's finger the moment she had entered her hand to put the bowl inside the cage. You could see the wounds on my mamma's ring finger.”

“Oh! Very bad”, I said to her but I really got pity for the parrot. At the same time, I felt jealous of Ankita that she had two parrots.

Ankita said to me happily, "I and my brother play a lot with parrots. We are very happy to get these parrots."

Listening to this, I stood up hurriedly. I didn't want to stay there any longer. It stirred me and aroused my desire to have pet enormously.

I made an excuse to take leave. I said to Ankita, "I have to complete my homework. So now, I am going to my house."

She didn't try to stop me either. I quickly rushed to my home. When I was on my way to home, parrot's screaming came to my ear. Having reached home, the first thing I did was that I requested mamma again for a pet. I said passionately, "Get me a parrot."

My words didn't sway mamma. She immediately said, "No, not at all. It cannot be fulfilled".

The price of freedom

My love for the pet went on mounting. Most of my friends had a pet, but I didn't have. I often dreamt of having a pet dog, cat or parrot.

My dream was not coming true. My friends were lucky. It was another shocking day for me. After returning from school, I went outside to play with friends. I learnt that one of my friends had brought beautiful birds. She lived opposite to my flat. I imagined the two sisters-Kaynat and Alina playing happily.

In the evening I went to her flat. I saw colorful birds in a cage lying in the balcony. There were a total of six birds. All of them were of a lovebird's size.

True to my imagination, I found both sisters very happy. They called the birds 'Love Birds'. The cage was beautifully decorated. There was a nest and tree trunk placed in the cage. Two small birds of light green and slate colour were quite gorgeous. Both of them were always entering into the nest and popping up heads outside. Sometimes, they were trying to sit on the tree trunk.

Suddenly, the younger brother of Kaynat and Alina moved near to the cage and opened the door. He pulled out the green bird hastily. The green bird screamed in pain. All birds got scared of sudden danger. In fear, they shuddered to the corner of the cage. Seeing all this flurry of activities, her brother began to laugh loudly. I did not like his demeanor. I left for my home at once.

I was sad. It was very much palpable in my face. So, when I asked mamma to bring a bird, she said to me for the first time, "If papa says okay, I do not have any objections."

The positive response from mamma lifted my mood to a great extent. I was sure that papa will fulfill my wish. I rushed to him and narrated the whole thing to Papa. Papa was kind enough to listen and said to me, "I will bring the bird when mamma agrees."

It was really good to hear at that time. I went to mamma and said to her that Papa has no issues. Mamma was a bit suspicious. She enquired what he had exactly told me. She wanted to know the specific sentence. When I told her, she made me understand what Papa had meant by saying so. Later, I realized that he had added conditions. I didn't understand at first that both of them were together in not fulfilling my wishes. They did not want to have a bird in the house.

Unaware of this, I still tried once more. I pleaded with mamma. She took a different course this time. She said, "You need to do one thing before bringing the bird to the house." She asked me to lock myself in a room for the whole day. The doors would be closed. I wouldn't get food and chocolates. I was not expected to come out of the room even once and not allowed to meet any person.

After thinking for a while if I would be able do so, I replied, "No, I can't live in a closed room even for an hour. It will suffocate me."

In fact, she wanted me to know how those birds and parrots would be feeling in a cage. She suggested me if I really wanted to see the bird and parrot and have love for them, I ought to go to the balcony or on the roof to watch them. I must get up in the morning and go to the park to watch them flying in open sky.

Her words fell flat on my ear. Later I thought,

“Mamma is right.” She also went on to tell me a mythological story. The story relates to Luv and Kush. The story has depicted stubbornness of Kush. It relates to the time when Mata Sita was staying with her son Luv & Kush in the Ashram of Maharishi Valmiki. One day, Kush wanted to keep some birds in the cage. Mata Sita kept Kush in a closed thatched hut. She gave him food and sweet dishes also, but didn't allow him to come out despite his continuous plead. After few hours, Kush had begun crying and requested Sita Mata to open the door of the hut. He also promised his mother never to ask for pet birds and said to her, “I know the price of freedom now.”

I had also come to know the price of freedom. But....I wanted to test it. The next day, I went to Ankita's home. I told Ankita about the previous day's incident occurred at Kayanat's home and Kush story as told to me by mamma. She heard it patiently. So, I said to Ankita, “Your parrots too, are feeling suffocated a lot in the cage. Please make them free.”

Ankita grimaced and appeared to be not listening to me.

I said to her, not out of jealousy, but I just wanted to see the power of the story which mamma had narrated to me. I asked her again to make parrots free. She got confused and came with a reason.

She said, "If she opens the cage and blows the

parrot, they may not be alive for long"

When I reasoned with her, she said, "They might have forgotten to fly after living in the cage for long time. The cat will catch them and eat them too."

She had a valid point. I also learnt from her that the birds' seller treats birds very badly. They keep them in filthy places. Birds are forced to eat their potty.

Meeting Bruzzo in Dharmshala

It was hurting to see people behaving badly to the innocent birds. Also, mamma's story on the issue of a pet had made me think otherwise. She had introduced me to the new world of nature. Now I had set out to look through the window to watch the birds and sometimes wake up in the morning with feeble sound whistle from the nearby small park.

I had almost forgotten about my deep earnest to have pets. The daily schedule of study, play and other activities had occupied me to a great deal.

However, there was something else to surprise me again. It is not easy to let the childhood's dream go unfulfilled. I got to appreciate it soon in the place called Dharmshala; a small town in the Kangra district of Himachal Pradesh. The place lies at the bottom of the Dhauladhar Mountains range and known to the world more for the famous spiritual guru Dalai Lama's residence, but it is also a heaven for birds.

I had an opportunity to visit here as my father got a teaching job at Central University of Himachal Pradesh, Dharmshala. Initially, there was an uncertainty in the family to move to this calm and quite city. My family members were divided to move over here from Delhi, but I wanted to come.

I asked Papa many a times, but he would keep silence all the time. He was reluctant to shift because of my studies. There were not many good schools here. Lastly, he had zeroed on Sacred Heart Senior Secondary School, Dharamshala. So, one day he said, "If you qualify in the entrance test, the family will move here." Luckily, I passed the exam and the decision was taken at last to move to Dharamshala. I saw many new birds for the first time. I saw them flying in the sky, chirping here and there. It was difficult to recognize many birds in the beginning.

And it is here I met the pet dog 'Bruzzo'. On June 8, 2020, we arrived Dharamshala. We had taken the first-floor of the house on rent. The landlord and landlady lived downstairs. They are an elderly couple. I call them uncle-aunty, because mamma called them so. A small pug, Bruzzo, also lived with them. The small dog was of silver fawn colour. His muzzle and eyes were black. For a few days, I only saw Bruzzo from distance. I never ever tried to go near him; forget to touch him.

One day I along with papa had gone to market for shopping and returned with plenty of chocolates and toffees. As soon as I entered the gate, Bruzzo rushed towards me. He saw me askance and came closer to me. He soon started sniffing my feet. I got nervous. Seeing this, aunty looked at me with love. She asked me, "Don't be afraid. Bruzzo wants to do

friendship with you."

I was panicky. Hardly had I paid attention to what she said. Seeing my uncomfortable condition, Aunty called Bruzzo and forbade not to touch me. Bruzzo stopped at once. Then, I saw him running away and went near to aunty. I took a sigh of relief and after that I came upstairs fast.

It was difficult to come to his term. I was hesitant to be friendly with him. The latest incident however made me to think about the friendship. When we returned from the market the other day in the late evening, Bruzzo ran towards me again. Papa was parking the car. I and mamma had opened the gate. I got scared to see Bruzzo in front of me. I ran and saw Bruzzo approaching my legs. Uncle came out and caught Bruzzo, before he could do any harm to me. I started breathing uncontrollably. I thought that Bruzzo has bitten me. But nothing like that had happened.

After that incident, I got afraid a bit more. I started to avoid Bruzzo. Whenever I had to get out of the gate, I asked aunty first to hold Bruzzo firmly.

After a few days, I and mamma started going for evening walk with aunty-uncle. It was summer then. Bruzzo also come along with them. One day uncle said to me, "You hold its leash."

At first, I hesitated a little... but I dared to hold his leash. He did nothing. Rather, he followed my ways and wishes, too. I really enjoyed holding it. Since then it turned out to be my routine. I became at ease with him.

One day I was spending leisure time with him, when he started to climb upon me. In fear, I called upon aunty. She was in the kitchen. Hearing me cry, she came out hurriedly. After instructing

Bruzzo not to disturb me, she handed over me some chocolates. She gave a piece of chocolate to Bruzzo as well. Aunty said Bruzzo wanted a pat on his back.

But whenever I tried Bruzzo had reciprocated to climb upon my feet. I wobbled and got scared. I was utterly confused if he really wanted me to love him or was angry with me. One day when I was standing next to him and trying to know his emotion, he farted stinking gas. The odour was so bad and intense that I could not stand there even for a second. I snapped my hand and became so upset. I came to my house and cleansed my face with soap. I changed my clothes as well. I came to know later that Bruzzo would do so when he used to eat heavy food. He would either vomit or passed such stinky gas, as aunty had told me.

The next day he behaved properly when I came to play with him. He did not try to climb upon me as though he might have sensed my uneasiness. In fact, we had started to understand each other. We both learnt to accommodate each other and spent time happily thereupon. The unique bond that developed between us was getting stronger day by day. In the following days, Bruzzo became my BFF i.e. Best Friend Forever.

Master for a day

Slowly and steadily, my attachment with Bruzzo grew up deeper. I would steal my time to play with him every day. I used to have long conversation with aunty and enquired a lot about Bruzzo. She would tell me his nasty acts in detail. She told me that it was not she but her daughter Meetu had bought Bruzzo. Bruzzo lived with Meetu in Chandigarh, but her landlord disliked him. He always put a ban on Bruzzo wandering here and there. He would ask Meetu to keep Bruzzo tied with leash in a room. Therefore, Meetu had left it here with aunty.

Poor Bruzzo! He had no choice. But in Aunty, he found a proper caretaker and also an opportunity of making new friends in Dharamshala. Aunty's grand daughter Atishi often comes to stay with her. She is a little cute baby and called Meetu, Meetu massi. So, I also started calling her massi. She is a loveable person.

Aunty told me numerous stories. How would she take care of Bruzzo? When it was severe cold in Dharamshala, they would go to Chandigarh just to provide a warmer environment to Bruzzo.

A very funny thing happened one day. Meetu massi is very fond of Bruzzo and used to him every day on video call. She would make a video call just to see him but all of a sudden, one day Bruzzo refused to show up his face. He was adamant. Despite repeated efforts made by aunty, he was not turning up in front of the mobile camera.

Aunty was puzzled to see this demeanour. But, when she said to Bruzzo, "Where is Tanishi?" He immediately looked up. She was stunned by this gesture.

When she told me I too was overwhelmed. Thereafter, I noticed, whenever aunty called my name, he always looked up anticipating that I would be there. Dogs are blessed with listening even low decibell sound as well. Whenever I would race on the floor, he would set out barking as if he was calling me downstairs. When I listened to it and reached near him, he would become so happy.

In happiness, he would protrude his tail. Also, whenever mamma screamed at me, he would show his resentment barking aloud. Probably, he was saying – Don't worry. I am standing downstairs to protect you.

Happy! Does happiness come all of a sudden? It was a very special day for me. Aunty called me and said to me, “We are going to Kangra today for the monthly health checkup. It will take four to five hours.”

She further added, “Take care of Bruzzo in a day time.” Handing over bananas to me, she advised me to serve it to Bruzzo after two hours.”

It was indeed a special delightful moment for me. I was supposed to be the master for the day. I tempted to jump out, but I anyhow managed my emotions. I was overjoyed thinking to be with Bruzzo for the whole day.

Fully engrossed in thought, I said to aunty, “Don't worry. I will take care of Bruzzo very well.”

Aunty had barely left the house and I went down to see Bruzzo for myself. I found him squat unpleasantly at the entrance looking outside. He didn't demonstrate any emotion even though I looked at him passionately. I didn't understand and returned, losing all my excitement, affection and joy for him. Soon, I realized he was very much sad. The whole premises seemed to take a forlorn look that day.

I however kept calling Bruzzo at every half an hour. After listening to my voice, he just looked upwards and then went up to the gate as if he was waiting for his master. It was surprising for me to see Bruzzo waiting for aunty. I gave Bruzzo a banana as I was instructed by aunty. He ate it but was not as fervently as he did before. I attempted to check with other seasonal fruits but to no avail. Earlier, the smell of banana made him run and he would relish it.

Unlike other dogs, he preferred to eat cucumber, pumpkin also. Surely, he loved to have Milk. Aunty-Uncle is a vegetarian, so Bruzzo did not get eggs or meat. It was only when Meetu Massi visited Dharamshala, she brought with her specially prepared feed for Bruzzo. Bruzzo liked that type of food very much. That day I had attempted to feed Bruzzo Banana, Biscuits and chocolates also. I had thought of enjoying the day a lot but it was sorry to see that he was not approving any of my gestures in the absence of his own master.

Bruzzo on vacation

After the health check-up, aunty returned in the evening. Bruzzo's sadness came to an abrupt end. I watched his change of mood. It reassured me seeing for myself he was alright.

Due to fear of corona and lockdown, I would not go to any other places. I either engrossed myself to study or played with Bruzzo. It was my favorite pass time. I would go downstairs hiding biscuits and bananas in my hand. Bruzzo always surprised me to find the same and chased until I would give him.

When I would take a long stride, he ran behind me. Sometimes, I started playing to keep the food items above his reach. He made efforts to catch it, but when failed to reach to a height; he would make a special sound, and it was then I obliged him to offer food items. He too enjoyed this game. Whenever I threw a piece of biscuit, he would run to pick it up. Sometimes, I befooled Bruzzo throwing a small stones instead. He would pick up pebbles in his mouth. Finding it hard, he would grimace his face. Sorry Bruzzo! When uncle or aunty patted on his head, he threw out the stone from his mouth. It was his favorite game too.

One day when I was playing with him, aunty told me all of a sudden that they were planning to go to their old house in the village for a few days. Their ancestral village was hundred kilometers away from Dharamshala. Bruzzo will also go there with them. It was nothing, but a big shock that I received. I become sad.

The next day, around 9 o'clock, uncle was driving the car out from the parking space. Bruzzo appeared as if he is not willing to go with them. He started running around the car. When all the stuff was kept in the car, he initially tried not to get into the car but. After a few minutes, he jumped inside

and sat on the back seat of the car.

When the car sped away, I had started feeling a big void. I missed Bruzzo a lot. In the evening when I was missing him, I called aunty on her mobile number and requested her to make a video call. Aunty made a video call. I saw Bruzzo in the courtyard playing with two small puppies. When I asked about it, aunty said to me, "There is a dogi near our house that has given birth to three puppies."

She further explained that the courtyard was not surrounded by a boundary wall. That's why the street dogs keep coming without any hurdle. I saw one puppy crossing the other side of the courtyard. The remaining two were happily playing with Bruzzo. The puppy's mother was not around. She had probably gone in search of food. After a while, the dogi came near puppies and started barking on Bruzzo. Bruzzo got scared and withdrew himself backwards. He turned his face towards me on the mobile phone and started barking in low tone as if he was also missing me. He recognized me, which was visible through his gait.

I was happy to learn that there were friends of Bruzzo in the village. The following day when I made a video call, I saw Bruzzo was running solitary in the entire courtyard. He sometimes started barking at once. At first, I was unable to know the reason but when I noticed that at a particular place only he was stopping for a while. I glanced through the frame and found that it was a parrot in a cage hanging in a house adjacent to the courtyard. Bruzzo ran near to the cage and then returned. He did this many times. He wanted me to notice the parrot.

Sometimes, he lay down on the grass spread in the courtyard. He appeared to be very cute. I was becoming impatient but there were no other options except waiting for Bruzzo to come.

Bruzzo is gone on vacations to another town with uncle-aunty. Therefore, for a few days, I have no stories to tell you about Bruzzo. Wait till he comes back! Till then, I would come with stories of other dogs like Alex, Munro, Lalu etc. In following chapters, you will come to know that despite feelings, love and care for dogs, why am I so scared of dogs?

When Alex scared me

Don't be sad. Bruzzo will come again. I know you too might be missing him. Let us start with another ferocious and lovely dog, Alex. Will you mind to recall that I lived in the housing society of Indirapuram, Ghaziabad? I assume no. It was there I had come across a shabby white dog, Alex. I still shiver to remember his ferocious look. He was of pomeranian breed. I had a chance to meet him when I was strolling in the park. Riya Didi, the owner of the dog, had brought it in the park.

You must be thinking, who is this Riya Didi? There was a girl named Ruby who helped my mamma in her domestic chores. She also stayed in my flat in day time and took care of me. She was very calm and a lovely girl. Ruby Didi was also hired by Riya Didi as a domestic help. Occasionally, she would get late and I used to go to Riya Didi's house to call her.

Ruby Didi had told me about the cute dog Alex in Riya Didi's house. My love for a pet made me foster a friendship with Riya Didi. She too reciprocated well. The dog Alex was very cute and charming. One day I asked Riya Didi to come with Alex in the park. She obliged me by bringing Alex out of the home with her, while I was taking a stroll in the evening.

All the other children were looking far away from Alex, as he came to the park. I went closer to him from behind. Alex was moving forward with Riya didi. Suddenly, he turned around and roared to scare me. My eyes caught this and I was fazed. Scared, I started to run away. That made Alex chase me, as it is said that dogs are quick to sense the fear in human being. I started crying mamma-mamma. Seeing Alex chasing me, I started screaming.

I thought he would bite my legs. After this, Riya Didi called loudly- Alex... Alex... When he heard it, he stopped, but I was crying. Then, all the children accompanied me up to the home. Alex did not bite me, yet I was crying.

My mamma was not present at that point of time in the house. She was in the office. When she returned home in the evening, I told her about the whole story. She helped me to come out of it. But, the fear lasted for long. After that, I was so scared of Alex that whenever I had to call my other friends in the society, I would make sure not to encounter with Alex. I would take a different and rather longer route. I avoided going in front of Alex. Instead of a short route, I would prefer to complete a round of the society.

The only solace for me was that when Riya Didi's mamma came to know about the incident, she started to keep Alex chained in home. I was so scared of Alex that when I was coming to Himachal, I did not bother to go to meet Riya Didi in her house. However, I had met Alex on his way back to home the previous day before I visited Himachal. But this time he was docile. Thank god. Now, I have memories of his two faces, one ferocious and the other kind one expecting friendship from my side. Now I realize that he was not so bad, but he needed a humanly touch from my side. Even today I remember that white and shabby dog Alex.

Munro, my friend for a day

Now, I introduce you to a very lovable dog Munro. She was older than me. The way she welcomed me into her house is very touching. Barely a month had elapsed and I was not able to come out from the unsavory memories of Alex. I met Munro at Shail Mathur's home, a good friend of mamma. We had visited her house in connection with interviewing one writer. She is a beloved one and of very helpful nature. I call her Massi.

As soon as I and mamma reached there and pressed the bell at the entrance of the house, Munro had rushed towards us. Shail Massi caught Munro firmly and we were waved to move inside the gate and taken to drawing room directly. Munro followed us and started smelling us lovingly. I was fearful for a while and regretted accompanying mamma to the place. It was like a nightmare.

Massi might have sensed my fear and she slid on the sofa next to me. Pointing to the Munro, she told that Munro was intending to make friendship with me. But I was so scared. She further told, keeping her hand on Munro, "This is your elder sister, Tanishi. It is 13 years old."

I was eight years old at that point of time. Slowly I

moved towards Munro, who tried to embrace me in anticipation that I had accepted her friendship. She looked genuine, lovely and cute. I forgot my earlier experience and got to mingle with ease. Munro took me to a round of the whole house. She truly

behaved like an elder sister. When she noticed the delay in serving snacks to me, she went to the kitchen and alerted massi to serve me fast. I was stunned to see this. I now call her Munro Didi. I was touched to the core.

Shail Massi is an animal lover. She told us about a snakelet was once seen in her courtyard. Instead of throwing it, she allowed and made a place for staying there. She also got to feed it from time to time. Small insects, eggs etc were its meal. Despite such hospitality, when the snake grew older, it went away from her house. I could not see that snake.

There was an aquarium also in her house. Munro did not make any issue with other such creatures. She knew well, I assume that she couldn't eat fish. After a while, when Munro became hungry, she went near to her bowl and started patting on it. It was nice to see and to be in the company of Munro didi. I enjoyed a lot while mamma was discussing story ideas and other things with her. Munro made the day special to me. She had made my day and roused my desire to raise a pet in my own house.

In the evening, we came back home. I started to rewind my time spent with her through snaps taken there. It has been my pasttime for some days.

Now, the clicked photos with Munro are my memoir only. When I was getting ready to come to Dharamshala in 2020, I called Shail Massi to know about Munro. She told with a heavy heart that Munro had passed away. It was hard to believe; listening to this the phone fell from my hand on the ground. Mamma asked me, "What happened?"

I was frozen for a while. When I told her about Munro, Mamma also became very sad. Recently, Shail Massi informed me that she had brought to home another cute dog that resembles Munro Didi. It might help Shail Massi to overcome her grief. She must be missing a lot, as the name of the new dog has also been christened Munro. You would love to know that both Munro didi and new Munro were street dogs. I am very happy to know that she looks like Munro. But no one can take place of Munro Didi.

Lalu! A notorious dog

Life is not like a smooth road. It has many bumps. After introducing you to a cute and loving dog, I embark you on a different journey. This is the story of a ferocious dog. His name is Lalu, lean and brown one. He is known for biting trespassers in the colony where we live in Dharamshala. I live near Himachal Pradesh Cricket Academy, Dharamshala. The place is called Dhauladhar Colony divided into three blocks. I live in 'A' block whereas Lalu lives in the 'C'block.

Whenever a person from another block or any other places goes to 'C' block, Lalu start barking first and finding a chance, he never misses to bite as well. He is well-known for his notoriety. Many a times, residents made up their mind to get rid of him. The other blocks people decided that Lalu should be transported to the shelter home of the stray animals or he should be left in the forest but to no avail.

An aunty of C block opposed the decision fiercely. Once people from an NGO had also come to take Lalu with them, but they had to abandon the plan due to aunty's strong objection. In fact, she had taken care of Lalu since its birth. She also gets Lalu

inoculated from time to time.

You might be wondering how I came to know about Lalu. I came to know because my father became his prey. He had gone for a walk in the 'C' block which is near to our block. Suddenly, a dog came near to him. First, he sniffed Papa's feet and then receded away. He had not gone far away. Papa didn't think of his return and went ahead with usual pace when suddenly felt piercing of teeth two or three times on his right leg. He turned around and what he saw was Lalu had done his job. Blood oozed out; thank god it was not oozing profusely, as he had worn that day a cotton trouser.

Papa came home hurriedly and having cleansed the blood with fresh water, he rushed to the hospital. He had to take five injections in a month at regular interval.

Luckily, Papa got the injections and he is fine now. It was a lesson for me. Whenever I see any dog in the street, first I make sure about the movement of a dog and keep a close vigil. It has helped me so far. One may be safe here with caution only, as there are many street dogs in Dharamshala.

Yes, you might be thinking, did I ever dare to go to 'C' block? No, not at all. I had never been in 'C' block all alone. It is not due to fear of Lalu, but as a precautionary step. Once accidentally I went to that side, I was very much scared though. Only a few days after biting Papa, I learnt that he had bitten a little girl too. A poor little girl! I feel pity for her. Lalu is very bad. He doesn't spare anyone even children.

The good solace is that he is a lion in his 'C' block only. His territory is confined. When he breaches it and comes out of 'C' block, all the other dogs of colony come together and show him his place. He retracts in a huff and goes back straight into his terrain.

Bruzzo returns

Yippi... Yahoo. Yes, after about a month Bruzzo had returned to Dharamshala. The moment I learnt that Bruzzo had come, I fastened my pace and descended the stairs in one go. It was a joy abound. I can't express it in words. Without saying Hello to uncle and aunty, I directly headed towards him and put my hand on the head of Bruzzo. He too seemed to be happy coming back to his original home. At the same time what I noticed was that Bruzzo was a little sluggish.

I enquired to his health. Aunty told that he had vomited in the morning. Uncle told me about Bruzzo's friends small puppies living in the village.

They were of black and white colour and growing fastly. It was evening when Uncle had reached Dharamshala driving himself and he was looking a bit tired too. Therefore, we didn't stay for long there. We stayed until they finished tea.

Asking them to get afresh, mamma requested for permission to leave. I too followed her even though I didn't wish to do so. I got another chance to meet when mamma went to give them food downstairs. Bruzzo was sitting in the verandah. He was gasping heavily. I gave him a biscuit to eat, but he didn't touch it.

Next day in the morning I had woken up early to go downstairs but when I reached there, I noticed no activities, I withdrew myself. It was now about half past eight, I went downstairs again. I had thought of Bruzzo would be alright and after taking proper rest in the night he would play the way he used to do previously. I tried thrice to play with him. But he disappointed me again and again.

I went to ask about Bruzzo's health from aunty. Aunty said to me, "Bruzzo is not eating food. He has got ticks and mice in his body. Usually, it catches in animals in village."

I came outside and gave him a biscuit, but he did not bother to eat it. Aunty had followed me. She pulled out ticks from his body and tried to make him feel better. I saw that from the skin where the ticks were removed blood was oozing off. I became worried for Bruzzo.

I came to my house and told mamma all that. Mamma also expressed her concern. I went downstairs a number of times that day just to see Bruzzo. He had however been sitting quietly the entire day. Aunty said that she had removed six ticks from its body. It seemed that Bruzzo had got infections from stray dogs. What I thought was that Bruzzo needed treatment.

Cloud of uncertainty

The next day early morning, I saw that Bruzzo was sitting in the car with uncle-aunty. They were going to the hospital. I felt happy to know, as the treatment would help him recover fast.

The whole day I missed him very much. I tried to concentrate but of no use. I had been waiting in the balcony. I saw uncle's car arriving from far away in the evening.I ran out and viewed that Bruzzo had come from the hospital. He got off the car slowly. Aunty told that he was given an injection. In the coming days, he would have to get more injections.

I saw that he was constantly bowing down his face. He sat down midway. All of us tried to feed him several times, but all efforts made were of no use.

He did not touch even his favourite fruit banana. Bruzzo was not the same now. He had lost his vigour. He was not active as well. Instead of playing, he had to follow the hospital regimen.

Bruzzo went to the hospital the following day too. That day he was administered two injections. This exhibited more adverse sign. When he returned home, he was vomiting for a while. Seeing the deteriorating condition of Bruzzo, aunty-uncle was upset too. They were worried if Bruzzo would be fit and healthy again.

They apprised their daughter Meetu Massi about the condition. Meetu Massi without wasting time came to Dharamshala from Chandigarh day after. She loved Bruzzo very much. When Bruzzo saw her, there was no limit to his happiness. Despite being seriously ill, he ran to see her. He climbed up on her and started moving his small tail. With gentle pat she said, "My child, now I have come to you. I will never leave you."

Bruzzo seemed to trust her words. She said, "Oh-oo.' You have a high fever. Still, you are showing yourself healthy."I saw that Meetu Massi washed her hand and went inside the house. Bruzzo, standing on the verandah, started tricking to go inside. He was repeatedly patting his claw at the door. He was crazy to go inside. After a while, he started barking. After some time the door was opened, he went inside.

He sat down on her lap. Her words truly worked.

Bruzzo didn't want to leave her. I called Bruzzo thrice but he did not even peep once. The second day in the morning, Meetu Massi took him for a bath. The doctor had suggested that if the fever was not coming down, he should take a bath. After bath, Bruzzo's health improved slightly.

I noticed that he was not paying attention to my voice those days. He was always roaming behind Meetu Massi. I became sad. I told all things to mamma. Mamma said, "Meetu has brought up him since childhood, that's why he considers her as his caretaker. He loves you too, but not as much as Meetu."

Then I made up my mind and consoled myself. Bruzzo's health was improving fast, but the doctor said that he is also growing older. So he may face all types of health problems. I thought that Bruzzo was just like that blossomed flower of which petals dries after some days. I started remembering those days when Bruzzo was active and used to roam behind me.

Bruzzo's interview

It was Meetu Massi's care and company that helped Bruzzo's health recovery fast. Though heavy medication had made him lazy, he was trying to be fit and healthy. I had a close eye on him as well. Of late, I wanted to know more about Bruzzo. So, it came to my mind to do Bruzzo's interview. He could not speak. Therefore, I decided to talk to his original owner Meetu Massi.

One day in sunny winter afternoon when I saw she was sitting in a chair in the lawn, I went to her and expressed my desire. She readily agreed to it. She was happy to talk about Bruzzo. I pulled another chair and sat beside her. When I began asking questions to her, I saw Bruzzo sneakily arrived near Meetu Massi. He sat down on her lap. It was a sight unforgettable. I moved ahead and first wanted to know about the real home of Bruzzo.

I asked, "Why did you decide to buy a pug?"

Meetu Massi, "Pug is a small dog. It can easily live at small places. It is quite cute too".

Me, "How much money did you spend for it?"

Meetu Massi, "I paid twelve thousand rupees. It was three years before i.e. in the year 2017. At that time Bruzzo was of only six months. No matter, how much money I had to spend; now I cannot live without Bruzzo."

Me, "But you live in Chandigarh, how do you manage to live without Bruzzo there?"

Meetu Massi, "You are right. I remember him all the time. After coming home from the office, I make a video call to mummy here and see his activities. I see him once every day. It is quite difficult to stay without him though."

Me, "Does it take too much time to attend Bruzzo's day to day activities like to clean him and etc?"

Meetu Massi,"No. I do manage time. To feed him, bathing, to take him on the walk, I do all chores of

Bruzzo with enthusiasm."

Me, "Do not you get annoyed doing all that like cleaning his potty and vomiting?"

Meetu Massi, "Not at all. The only thing which I dislike is that he falls sick, I do not like it."

Me, "Has Bruzzo tasted non-vegetarian food ever?"

Meetu Masi, "He wants to eat non-veg. When he passes from the egg-omelette shop, he craves for that. He does not want to move from there. I give him occasionally boiled eggs or omelette. Non-veg remains are there in his feed too. He also eats bones prepared by eggs and chicken syrup."

By the time Meetu Massi finished this sentence, I had observed Bruzzo trying to leave the interview. Seeing this, I also decided to end the conversation. I had already known most of Bruzzo's habits of eating and others. So I decided not to ask any further questions.

Meetu Massi told me Bruzzo's childhood story. Bruzzo was just 2-3 months, when she had brought it home. After bringing Bruzzo home, she made him take bath to remove dirt from his body. She said that after the bath, Bruzzo had got fever. She then took Bruzzo to the doctor who suggested for washing Bruzzo after three months as Pug is a very delicate animal. Meetu Massi further said, "You should know a very interesting fact about Bruzzo." In the beginning, Bruzzo didn't recognize his name. When she called Bruzzo by his name, he would see towards her. She would get annoyed to see this gesture. Slowly, Bruzzo learnt his name and all other things.

Bruzzo initially liked to live with Meetu Massi most of the time. He kept following her everywhere. One morning I saw that Meetu Massi was sleeping in her room. Bruzzo sat outside the door just like a bodyguard to her. He was not allowing anyone to go into the room. Uncle wanted to go to the room for some work, but he was forced not to go. He kept standing in front of him. Bruzzo is an animal so he can't speak. If he could speak like a human, he would have said, "She is sleeping. Do not go inside the room."

Encounter with Mithoo the Rabbit

Bruzzo's health was improving. Meetu Massi's companionship had made him smart too. He had learnt to tease others. Bruzzo would play tricks to get more attention. One day I touched him with love. He got irritated. He wanted to inspect me and test my love for him. But I should learn to distinguish between tricks and his bad mood. At times when he was not in a good mood and if someone touched him, he would get angry easily. Bruzzo annoyed me too. Since this incident I became cautious. I touched him very carefully.

The second thing was that whenever I touched him, some hairs of his body would come in my hand. I noticed it and shared with Meetu massi who ascribed it to the ticks. His hair was weak and had started falling off.

Time was running fast. About two months had passed by. Bruzzo was not as friendlier to me as he used to be. He was not playing with me any longer. He did not respond to me at times. I felt very bad, but I knew that he was an animal. He will not understand my emotional stirring. That's why I had started making some more animals as my friends.

In Dharamshala I have a friend called Niharika. I had met her at the general store where she used to come to buy Chips and Chocolates. One day she said to me, “Did you know that I have a rabbit at home.”

I said, “No, you never told me about that.”

"Anyway, what is the name," I asked.

She promptly said, "His name is Mithoo. If you want to see it, then come to my house."

It was a pleasant surprise for me. It was the time when pandemic covid 19 1st phase was passing over. Lockdown was lifted. I went to her house in eagerness to see Mithoo. Soon, it became routine. Mithoo was a white rabbit with red eyes. He was a bit shy too. Whenever I wanted to touch him, he would run away. One day Niharika put Mithoo in a basket and she came to my home.

Bruzzo saw Mithoo for the first time, so he had begun barking. But Mithoo unscared went near him and what transpired between both of them is unknown. What I observed they became fond of each other in short span of time and behaved like a good friend.

In nature's lap

The colony we live in Dharamshala is quite calm and open. To the right side next to our house is empty patch of land. A huge farmland lies behind my house in which vegetables and other seasonal crops are grown. There are Cedar and Pine trees along the edge of the farm. I am developing an interest in these things for the first time, as in Delhi I hardly had got an opportunity to see these things.

Though I belong to a farmer's family, I had not been in the village for a long time. I remember I visited only twice grandpa's home Maksudpur in the Gaya district of Bihar. Of course, I also belong to this same village. Now I will try to go there more often. I might be 5 years old when I had visited village for the first time. It was a new experience for me to look around farmland and observe crops growing therein. The natural flora and fauna were also along the roadside.

It was pleasant to see the vegetables in the field. We would eat vegetables before but I was completely ignorant of how it was cultivated in the field. The curiosity helped me widen my horizon. Many topics of life sciences are easier now, for me, to understand. The things changed and become far better now.

The interest developed then was now acquiring a new meaning to me. Here, I also got familiar with the variety of animals. Cow, bulls, dogs, mongoose and different types of birds used to come to the empty tract of land next to our house. One day I saw a bull stirring green grass there. In the beginning, I misunderstood it as a cow. When mamma told me, then I understood to distinguish. I kept the name of that bull-Moti. I often offered Moti bread, vegetables' peel etc. He liked cabbage peels very much.

In Dharamshala, eagles are also in plenty. They keep flying above roof all day. I desired to make them my friend in the beginning. I waved holding bread in my hand. Mamma saw me doing so one day and she cautioned me in time. She said that it could be dangerous. Seeing the food in your hand, the eagle can even bite your head. I got scared and stopped the practice forthwith.

Many birds, like Bulbul, Rüfous treepie, Sparrow, Humming Bird, Parrot, Cuckoo, Myna, Great barbet, owl etc are also frequently spotted in this area. Some birds would come on my terrace as well. I made it a rule to give them food grains. Owls often appeared in the evening. One day an owl was buzzing like horror voices sitting on the tree near the window of our bedroom. I had downloaded Birds App that helped me to identify many birds based on their voices. I recognized many unknown birds living around us through the App only. One day I also saw an Indian Pond Heron, which was flying with a lizard in her beaks. I also saw white-throated Kingfisher.

Of late, I had reduced my time to see birds daily, as my Unit Test examination of school was scheduled in a fortnight. I was feeling a bit guilty not to give them food grains daily. Meantime, I read the book 'Birds in your backyard and beyond' which mentions that birds became lazy if someone provides them food. I was in dilemma when my

examinations were over. I was thinking about how to pass time so I resumed meeting Bruzzo every day. Surprisingly, he began to pay more attention to me now. I was very happy to see that after such a long time Bruzzo again had moved closer to me. I slowly caressed her forehead. He moved his head in a way as if he was asking me – why did not you come to meet me for so many days?

My first birthday in Dharamshala

Today is a special day for me. It's not only chapter 17. My birthday falls on October 17. Guess how old I am now? Forgot it... Don't worry... Go back to the blurb and read the author's intro. Yes, I am 10 now. This is my first birthday in Dharamshala. I am missing my Delhi friends a lot. Anyway, I am very happy. I am celebrating my birthday and had cut my first cake at midnight yesterday i.e on 16th October. And I was overwhelmed by receiving a lot of gifts from Mamma and Papa.

In the evening I had plans to celebrate the birthday party with my new friends at home. I had been busy since morning decorating the house as per my choice. Meetu Massi also had come upstairs and helped decorating our home with balloons and other materials. She had closed the entrance gate of the upstairs so that Bruzzo couldn't turn up.

It was not liked by the Bruzzo. He was barking continuously as long as Meetu Massi stayed upstairs. He scratched the gate many times from his claws. He, however, got an opportunity to sneak in once accidentally someone had left the opened the gate. He was smart enough to make his way upstairs. He was happy now to be here. He wandered here and there.

In the evening, when the cake was about to cut, all people assembled on my floor by closing the gate. Poor Bruzzo was alone. I was thinking of him while cutting the cake.

Suddenly, what I saw Bruzzo had appeared in front of us. I was happy to see him. I fed him a piece of cake with my hand. In fact, one of my friends had

come up and he had forgotten to close the gate. Bruzzo got the chance to come upstairs and eat cake also. Meetu Massi ran to catch him. He then got away from her grip. He roamed around the house. Seeing his activities, all of us laughed very much. Some guests were afraid of him as well. The poor Bruzzo was caught at last. Meetu Massi lifted her in the lap and went downstairs. On the day of my Birthday, Bruzzo had made everyone laugh with his playful activities.

Friends in Dharamshala celebrated my birthday and made it a memorable one. But, I want a gift from you too; my dear readers. Do complete reading the book and send me your feedback. I will be happy to read all of them. Thank you for having patience up to now.

Atishi loved Bruzzo too

Of late, Bruzzo had become naughty and moody too. It was partly because of Atishi. You might be thinking who she is. Just recall the chapter why do I call Meetu Massi. Yes, Atishi is Meetu Massi's elder sister's daughter. Atishi is 8 years old. She lived in Hamirpur, about 100 km away from Dharmshala. She comes to Dharmshala at her Nani's house and stays here for a month and go back.

She is jovial. She can make fun out of anything. She does not hesitate to tease Bruzzo. One day what she did was undesirable. She kicked Bruzzo with her feet. But Bruzzo did not do anything to her. She took it granted forever. She would sit on Bruzzo's back. I wondered seeing love and care of Bruzzo for Atishi. One day, she kicked Bruzzo again. This time Bruzzo was not so kind. He got irritated and scratched her legs with his nails. Meetu Massi came immediately and saved the pity girl from a big danger.

Thereafter Atishi, however, mend her ways. She would behave now properly with Bruzzo. She would also give chocolates and toffees to Bruzzo. She was full of pranks. She also devised a method to play with Bruzzo. She made Bruzzo run behind herself by showing grains of peas in her fist. Bruzzo had to follow her for a long. Sometimes, she would give and the other time she just befooled throwing away the small ball. Bruzzo however, loved the mischief. Bruzzo then used to play with the ball.

The most fun was to see Bruzzo stand on his two feet when Meetu Massi asked him to stand up and do so. The other Bruzzo's favorite game was that he picked up the pebbles lying near the flower pots. When aunty or uncle would see this he would hide. Aunty held his head delicately and put a finger in his mouth to remove stone pieces. I think he

misunderstood the stones to be peanuts. Bruzzo liked peanuts too much. He would take peanuts in the mouth, peel off the peanuts and swallow the same. I still remember the day of Lohri, how he was placing his feet on burning log of wood to eat peanuts. Though everyone else laughed at him, he moved around the fire with us.

Fights with the disease

The doctor's diagnosis was coming to be true. Bruzzo was getting sick day by day. He had to fight one disease after another. He had to stay in Dharamshala in this severe winter. The pandemic corona had his winter vacation cancelled to Chandigarh. The severe cold and laziness on the part of Bruzzo had adverse effects on his health. Everyone was trying to make Bruzzo healthy and happy.For Bruzzo, Meetu Massi bought online some winter dresses. Bruzzo looked very cute in the blue and red sweater and woolen pants. Cold had its impact on him

According to the age of Bruzzo, his weight was relatively high. He was four years plus. His weight varied ten to twelve kilos. To reduce weight, it was necessary to take him for morning and evening stroll daily. But now, the winter had its peak, the unpleasant time in Dharamshala. It remains very chilling cold in December-January. Bruzzo was feeling it badly. He often sat down in front of aunty's heater.

He got severely sick again. He was taken to the hospital immediately. Timely treatment worked to certain level. Bruzzo was showing slow recovery.

The side effect of the three injections had its toll on his vigour and vitality. He had lost his appetite. He would prefer to eat food of his choice.

Bruzzo liked sweet things very much. The adverse impact was that his hair had begun to fall off again. His legs also got several wounds and healing was

not up to mark. It was a sign of worrying. Because of this, I also hesitated to give biscuits to him. In those days, Meetu Massi was taking care of him. She had got some special types of feed for Bruzzo. She would give that feed to serve Bruzzo, whenever I play with it. I would feed him. I would put one-two pieces in front of him.

Bruzzo was taken to the hospital alternate days. The doctor would examine him thoroughly and prescribed lots of medicine and ointment. The ointment was regularly applied on the wounds by Meetu Massi. Due to the medicine, the wounds of his feet got cured and hair falls were stopped. Ticks also disappeared with the help of medicines. Seeing the improvement in the health of Bruzzo, I got some relief.

Golden retriever's friendship

It was 18th January 2021. Meetu Massi and aunty had come to our house for BP checkup about 8 o'clock in the night. We have a digital blood pressure machine at home. I was watching a cartoon serial on TV and laughing loudly. When both of them entered into our drawing-room, I requested them to sit down on the sofa. In the meantime, mamma also came there. She asked both of them for tea.

Bruzzo was barking downstairs. Meetu Massi in the middle of conversation asked me, "Let's go for a walk. After informing mamma I went for a walk with her. Bruzzo was doing loo at every wall and near the parked car. He stopped at a place and did his potty too. He, at times, smelled a kind of grass.

I was in a sleeper and was not in a very comfortable dress at that time. We both were not even wearing masks. That's why we decided to return home early. Having completed two rounds of the colony, we came home back.

On my way back to home I recalled those summer days when I used to hold the leash of Bruzzo. They were golden days. I used to wait for the evening. At that time Bruzzo was also healthy. Now he was often getting sick. Old memories flashed back when Bruzzo would get tired and refused to move further. He stood at one place. It made us return home.

Now the things had changed completely. He ate very little food and vomit it in a short while. It meant that he was still not completely well. Despite all efforts made by Meetu Massi, he was not getting rid of the disease. Meetu Massi was making a lot of sacrifices though.

Meetu Massi had once told me the Pug breed does not live without its owner. They feel very lonely and insecure as well. The feeling that the owner has left might make the pug sick.

It was true in case of Bruzzo. I had noticed it many times. When Meetu Massi would go to the market or any other places, Bruzzo appeared to be very sad. He disliked eating in her absence. And sitting near the gate, he looked outside in anticipation of her early arrival.

The only thing he did was that if a dog or unknown person passed near the gate, he would start barking. After this, he would be silent. And at regular interval, he went to the room of Meetu Massi and sat on her bed for a while. Pug doesn't afford to combat or confront. Bruzzo liked to play with other street dogs but from distance. When dogs came in front of the gate, he used to come towards the gate and peep from inside only.

Pugs are just like a decorative item. They love human being. So was the case with Bruzzo. When people are around him, he used to bark looking at any unknown person. When there was nobody at home, Bruzzo kept looking at the gate quietly. If an unknown person opened the gate and entered the house, he would be silent instead of barking or sniffing them.

We would go for a walk in the evening. What I had observed is that when Bruzzo was with uncle and aunty, he presented himself to be ready to fight any outside dog. Uncle used to send off the stray dogs with stick and protect Bruzzo. All these actions of Bruzzo were very funny.

To express his happiness, he stood on his two legs or started barking in soft tone. One day, Bruzzo was running hurriedly towards the gate. I also ran behind him. I saw that a friend of Bruzzo was standing the other side of the gate. It was Golden Retriever. This is also a species of dog. Bruzzo started to scare him. Retriever however wanted to do friendship with him. After some time both began to bark together. This means that both of them have become friends.

Bruzzo meets Labrador

It was another fine Sunday morning for me. Not morning, the clock had struck fifteen past nine when Meetu Massi called me and proposed to go for a long walk. She said to me, “Would you like come along with me for the morning walk?”

I said in a huff, “Yes, I am coming downstairs after fifteen minutes.”

I had woken up late. It takes me usually 15-20 minutes to freshen up. I brushed my teeth, gulped milk, got ready and came down hastily. Bruzzo was having milk in his bowl. Seeing me, he tried to sip fast. Due to that he pulled down the utensil. Milk spread all over the floor. I could not see it and

slipped on the ground. It was irritating but I looked around to make sure if there was anyone present or not. I found nobody except Bruzzo. Being an animal he could not tell anything to anybody.

Meetu Massi came out and we went out for the walk. I and Meetu Massi were talking only about Bruzzo. What I saw suddenly was a bull in front of us. I said aloud, " Oops! How did it come at once?" Bruzzo too was shocked, but this time he put up a brave posture. Bruzzo didn't scare at all. He barked until the Bull made his way in other direction.

Hardly had we walked 50 steps, we saw a Labrador dog. It was Bruzzo who saw it first. He alerted us by barking. In return, he started barking too looking at Bruzzo and appeared the fight was imanent. I got afraid also. Luckily there was a stick in my hand. When I cracked it at the poles, he retracted. Bruzzo was not alone. He was with us. So he wanted to fight with dog. Meetu Massi pulled his leash and then we could move further.

On our way back, Meetu Massi told us about an Animal Translator App. I was puzzled to imagine how that could be true. I downloaded the app after reaching home. It was very funny. It tells the language of animals in Hindi or English. I also came to know how animals talk among themselves. Can it help human beings to understand? Is it right or wrong? I asked myself. Anyway, I recommend to use it just for fun.

Animals share their feelings too

It was papa's holiday today. We had gone for shopping. After coming back when I and Papa entered the home, I found mamma and aunty engaged in gossip. I went near Bruzzo. Meetu Massi was slowly patting his head.

It was winter time. They all were enjoying the sunlight in the noon. I had tried my hand on the translator app previously. But I wanted to be more familiar with it. I asked Meetu Massi to help me use the animal translator app to Bruzzo.

She was having her phone and gave me hands on training. Some boys were making clamour outside. Bruzzo began to yap at them. Meetu Massi recorded the voice of Bruzzo. She then transferred it to the animal translator app, to know the meaning of Bruzzo's voice.

What did he want to say? Imagine!

It was beyond imagination. Bruzzo was saying - look at my beautiful face. Look at my body. I am smart. We all started laughing at this translation. This means that Bruzzo is proud of his beauty. Therefore, instead of saying them to reduce noise level, he was asking to behold his beauty.

It was amazing to know. The other day I was reading the book 'Children's Knowledge Bank'. There was a chapter on the conversation of animals. It was mentioned that the animal cannot talk like us. The size of their brain is quite small. They do share their feelings with other animals in their unique manner.

When any bird looks at a cat, it starts to twitter loudly. By doing so, it expresses its fear. Through this, it also makes vigilant to other companion bird. This is the law of nature. When the dogs are angry, they start barking. So the translator app may be right or wrong too. There are many positive reviews about animal translator. We should not be in this confusion that what is right and what is wrong? We should use it just for fun.

The Children's Knowledge Bank also made me understand... Why does a dog bite? The book is informative and talks about different aspects. If the dog bites someone then the viruses spread into the whole body. The virus is called Rabies. It is also written that if the dog gets infected with Rabies, it becomes mad. It dies within 3 to 5 days. The dog dislikes eating anything at that time. The saliva of its mouth continues to be flows out. It is very dangerous. So, it is advised to get the pet dog vaccinated. Bruzzo has got Rabies vaccine.

Lovely Puchuu

I have earlier mentioned that there was a general store near our house. I used to go there to buy all my favorite things like chocolates, toffees, maggie, biscuits, snacks and Juices. On the way to the general store, there was a house, which had wide open space inside the boundary. Near this house lived a dog. Any disturbance in her activities would mean invite her wrath. Her voice was dominating. I called her Lucky.

She had given birth to four lovely puppies. One day I had bought something from the general store. On my way back to home I stayed for a while to watch those pretty puppies. Lucky from distance stared at me, she started groaning. She behaved as if I had come to take her puppies. I got scared and left the place hastily taking a long stride.

The next day I saw that Lucky was giving training to puppies, how to catch prey or search for food on their own. Lucky would bring some food items, and then it was distributed by her. All the children got food alternately. Sometimes she only watched her puppies finding food items. One of them a little bigger one would come to our gate. I would give bread. But, when I attempted to go closer, then it would run away. I called it Puchuu. I left something for it to eat every day.

All of a sudden, Puchuu was not visible for few days. I always thought that she might have gone somewhere or her mother might have prohibited her to come here. One day when I got out of the house, I saw that Puchuu was sitting near a scooter. I called her...Puchuu. But she ignored. I thought that Puchuu had forgotten me. She was engaged in arranging her food.

The other day I gave bread to another dog. He ate and left something. When he went away, Puchuu came and started eating crumbs of bread. I was very happy to see her. I ran to the house and got tasty bread. When I came with bread, Puchuu ate it. I loved Puchuu very much, but did not know why she was not coming. After some days, she had started coming to my house and loved to eat whatever I offered her. Some days later, she would come at exact 4 pm. And I used to serve her food.

Mamma said to me, "To get the puppies to feed milk, mother too needs to be fed well"

I took it seriously. Whenever lucky or puchuu came near my gate, I was ready to give milk to her in a bowl. There was a strange thing about Puchuu that she could not eat stale bread. She would eat fresh bread only. Sometimes, Puchuu outside and Bruzzo standing inside the gate happily licked each other's mouth through the gap of the grills.

She has vanished again for some time. Let us see when she starts coming back, the moody dog. Another dog, I named her Flora has also become friend of mine in these days. She comes just for food sake. She is brown in colour and of serious nature. She keeps herself busy with her puppies. Sometimes, she sleeps on the road itself.

The news of Bruzzo going to Chandigarh

We all love dogs. They are loyal to us. They know their limits. They are also very particular about their territory. Some days ago, a new dog came near to my house. It's colour was brown and black. Seeing the new dog, the dog of my block thundered a sound of alert and in a few seconds, many street dogs got assembled and started barking loudly.

They were very ferocious and ready to pounce upon the pity new dog. The new dog was a pet and he had lost his way. He was wagging his tail. It appeared the big fight was immanent, if uncle hadn't intervened in time with the stick. He stroked repeatedly thump on the ground and struggled hard to save the pet from street dogs.

Good luck prevailed. The pet was rescued by making a way to escape him. He trudged his way in fear realizing his mistake. In hilly areas, it is common practice that people keep street dogs as a pet in their home which sometimes plays escape from the owner. They fail to know that they shall not be welcome in the street dogs' company.

My neighbour had also made a white lovely dog as a pet when he was too small.

As the puppy grew up, he was cute, slim and very active. Often, he crossed the front of my house doing some mischief. He sometimes barked at innocent Bruzzo. If he had a chance to fight, he would have sure indulged in it. He was good looking but bad at heart. Even when Bruzzo was not in the sight, he would woof at times looking askance inside the gate.

This gesture was detested by Bruzzo. He used to revert yowling in equal measure with a deep desire in his heart to beat it in the fight despite the fact his health was deteriorating fast.

The treatment of Bruzzo was going on. Initially, it was assumed he had become weak and get over it

with the passage of time. When it didn't work, he was shown to another doctor. His diagnosis and prescribed medicines also made a slight improvement at the beginning of treatment. Both doctors had examined him thoroughly but they were unable to find a definite cure of his illness. Meetu massi had become very much concerned about it. She wanted better treatment of his undiagnosed disease.

One day I went downstairs and gave biscuits to Bruzzo. He didn't touch it. I enquired to Meetu Massi who was sitting perplexed there. She might be thinking of the options of the treatment available. She knew I loved Bruzzo too much. Instead of answering my question she at once said, "Love Bruzzo. Feed him. You might not get more opportunities to play with."

I was flabbergasted. I was confused about what to say, I fumbled to ask her, "Why are you saying such things?" Meetu Massi sensed my concern and said, "Nothing to worry about. I am thinking of Bruzzo to take to Chandigarh with me for the treatment".

It did not please me. I was even more stunned to hear this. I started remembering all the stories; the moments I had spent with him flashed through my mind—one after another—since Bruzzo had met me for the first time. How did we become good friends? Whenever mamma scolded me, he would begin to bark and came near to stairs.

Also, it was true that I was worried of his deteriorating health. I went through mixed feelings. I felt sad because he was going. I was happy because he will get better treatment.

My friend Chiya

The very think of parting anybody is very painful. The next day there was another shocker for me. I had just woken up in the morning. Papa was talking over the phone and after some time, he handed it to mamma. I asked him, "Who is on the line"

He said sadly, "Chiya's papa is talking to mamma"

I saw mamma was also expressing grief and reassuring him over the phone. I heard her saying that it was a thing not in the control of human beings. I failed to guess what had exactly happened. Hurriedly, I went to the drawing-room and asked papa, "What have happened to Chiya's papa."

He said to me, "Chiya's dadaji is no more. He left this human body for the heavenly journey."

It was unbelievable. I felt bad. I had started understanding the pain of loss in the family members.

I was the witness of my family grief and sorrow when choti dadi had passed away in November last year. My dadaji has four brothers. My dadi is the elder one and dadi number 2 had also passed away some times back. Since November 2020, it was the fourth death in three months that I had come to know in the family or friend's family. The other day I woke up and found my dadi was crying as her sister had died. I found dadi that time shaken from inside. Though she is a strong lady, the pain of losing her own was visible on her face. The third death had occurred in my village Maksudpur, Gaya in Bihar where I belong to.

Before that, I was naive about what the death of kith and kin brings with it. In October last year (2019), when my choti dadi number 4 had died just a few days before my birthday i.e. 17 October. I had become sad because my birthday celebration was cancelled last year. It was etched in my mind the death begets cancellation of celebrations only. Then I saw mamma in extreme grief when her mamu –Meero Mamu had passed away. But, I was unsure of the reason for the pain. This time the incidents of demise in a row made me think and now I had somewhat understood its effect on near and dear one.

While these incidents flip in my mind one after another, I thought of how Chiya might be feeling. Of late she had got very attached to her dadaji. She had mentioned it in our evening conversation. She had been living with him for the last six months in Dehradun. She was there because of the pandemic, as her father was working from home and school was closed down. Chiya is a good friend of mine. Chiya and her mamma-papa and my family are friends for a long time. They lived in the Patrakar Vihar society. Chiya, aunty and uncle had come to Dharamshala as well in June and stayed with us for fifteen days. It was Chiya who made me settle here. We played a lot in those days. When she was leaving for Dehradun, I had become very much emotional. I had even extracted a promise from them to come here in December.

Now December was over. I had asked many times papa if they would come. He would say sure. Contrary to that I asked papa this time, "We shall go to Dehradun."

Papa said, "Let us see what we shall do?"

I asked, "Why?"

He said so because dadi was not feeling well those days. She was having dizziness. While she would get up from bed, she was having a feeling of falling off. In such a situation it was not possible to go anywhere.

Papa was unable to make up his mind at the outset. Later, it was decided that mamma and I would go. Mamma and I went to Dehradun in the car for two days. When I met Chiya I was relaxed. I saw that there was a gathering of all her family members to perform the traditional rites haven.

In two days short stay in Dehradun, I had forgotten Bruzzo. In return journey only, it came to my mind that Bruzzo might have gone to Chandigarh. Surprisingly, when I reached home I saw Bruzzo here.Meetu massi had changed her mind, as the private cab didn't allow taking the dog along with! It was a respite for some time. I also came to know that when I was not here, Bruzzo had missed me a lot. Whenever aunty asked him, "Where is Tanishi?" He looked towards the gate. Previously he looked towards the balcony.

The final day

Bruzzo lived here for almost one and a half months thereafter. In those days, I tried my best to spend free time with him. I observed different shades of him. Time had played its role. Bruzzo was a bit less naughty and more mature. I had made up my mind to spend the entire day with him; the day before he was supposed to go to Chandigarh. That day finally arrived.

I went downstairs in the morning and it was a pleasant surprise to see Bruzzo all alone. Meetu massi and the whole family had gone somewhere for some time. Almost two hours, I had full choice to have fun with him. I fed him a biscuit, his feeds and also calcium biscuits as I was instructed earlier by Meetu massi.

Despite my unit test scheduled the next day, I spent most of the day with him. Of late, I had developed a special bond and felt a void in his absence. Bruzzo too would reciprocate his love in abundance. One day when I was playing badminton with Papa, my shuttle had landed in the adjacent house premises. When I went to fetch that, Bruzzo came to the gate following me. The other incident which had touched me the most was his bold act of protecting

me putting his own life in danger. One day I was playing outside the gate in the street. I was fully engrossed in the game. I did not notice the car coming from behind was likely to hit me. All of a sudden, Bruzzo came near my feet and started howling. I turned back to see the car which was about to hit me. I immediately jumped aside. Bruzzo had intervened in time and protected me.

True to his goodness, Bruzzo had returned my past help by saving my life. I recalled the episode when Bruzzo was encircled by stray dogs one day. The gate was left open by the uncle. I was looking at Bruzzo from my balcony. What I saw was that he had gone out all alone. The four street dogs resting at some distance were in jerk got ready and moved ferociously towards him. I immediately called Meetu Massi loudly and informed her about Bruzzo's devil dares. I rushed to help Bruzzo. Meetu Massi followed me and raised a stick in her hand

and made street dogs go away and saved Bruzzo by lifting in her lap. Thus, Bruzzo was saved from the stray dogs.

By the way, the day had finally arrived when Bruzzo was ready to go to Chandigarh. I wanted to be with him the last day as well but I had a unit test. That's why I could not spare much time during the day. In the evening, aunty called me downstairs and said to me, "Bruzzo is going."

Though I knew he had to go, it was no less than a big shock to me. I was not ready to listen to it. It made me dumb for a while. It was 9 o'clock at the night. I saw that Bruzzo too was not willing to go but he had anticipated a tacit plan for himself. While he was leaving, he was somber, went inside the car without a fuss and sat quietly beside Meetu Massi.

He seemed to be very comfortable in the cab, he was pained and very sad. I was told by aunty later that whenever my name was called out, he would plunk to the door side. He was upset and not eating properly. He did not have anything on his way to Chandigarh. It meant he was also missing all of us.

I always miss Bruzzo. Nobody does follow me now when I go downstairs. The time spent with him is my memories trove. I keep inquiring about him from Aunty. Once I had a chance to see him in a video call. He was sleeping in front of the cooler. In Chandigarh, it is very hot in the month of June. I have learnt that he makes excuses to go to the bathroom to avoid heat. He enjoys cold air by sitting in front of the AC or the cooler. Some days back, he was very sick. He is getting treatment there in a big hospital. He has to visit doctor at six days intervals. Bruzzo lost his two teeth recently when he was chewing toffees. I hope he will be fine soon and we will see each other, but I do not know I will ever meet Bruzzo or not.

When Bruzzo ignored me in the past, I would consider I should stop writing about my good days spent with him. After seeing his innocence, I would

start writing my memoirs. I knew that I would write memoirs someday but it was not thought of that it would be completed so soon. Anyway, it will not make any difference to him. His cuteness always melts my heart.

Tanishi Sharma is studying in class six at Sacred Heart Senior Secondary School, Dharamshala in Himachal Pradesh. Her love for stories is profound.

From her early childhood, she started writing and telling stories to others. She is a recipient of first prize in storytelling in class 1 at DPS Gautam Buddha Nagar, Uttar Pradesh where she studied up to 4th Standard. She does book review and storytelling on a YouTube channel 'Amazing Books'. She also does live storytelling on her mamma's Facebook page *Shabdon ka Safar*.

A YouTube channel has also interviewed her for regularly uploading book reviews. She is the youngest book reviewer. Presently she is working on another book.

Stuti Maheshwari lives in a small city Amroha in Uttar Pradesh. Stuti received first prize in regional level art competition conducted by Moradabad mandal when she was studying in class 8th. Since childhood, she has penchant for Arts and received many prizes for Mehendi art.

Presently, she is a commerce student of class 12th in Blue Birds International School, Mandi Dhanaura in Uttar Pradesh.